Francis Frith's 50 CLASSICS

RAILWAYS

The Francis Frith Collection

First published in the United Kingdom in 2004 by
The Francis Frith Collection®

Reprinted in 2005
ISBN 1-85937-903-6

British Library Cataloguing in Publication Data

50 Classics - Railways
Compiled by Terence Sackett and Julia Skinner

The Francis Frith Collection®
Frith's Barn, Teffont,
Salisbury, Wiltshire SP3 5QP
Tel: +44 (0) 1722 716 376
Email: info@francisfrith.co.uk
www.francisfrith.co.uk

Printed and bound in Malta

Front cover: CORSHAM, Box Tunnel 1904 51492
The colour-tinting is for illustrative purposes only, and is not intended to be historically accurate.

AS WITH ANY HISTORICAL DATABASE THE FRITH ARCHIVE IS CONSTANTLY BEING CORRECTED AND IMPROVED AND THE PUBLISHERS WOULD WELCOME INFORMATION ON OMISSIONS OR INACCURACIES

FRANCIS FRITH
VICTORIAN PIONEER

Francis Frith, founder of the world-famous photographic archive, was a complex and multi-talented man. A devout Quaker and a highly successful Victorian businessman, he was philosophic by nature and pioneering in outlook. By 1855 he had already established a wholesale grocery business in Liverpool, and sold it for the astonishing sum of £200,000, which is the equivalent today of over £15,000,000. Now in his thirties, and captivated by the new science of photography, Frith set out on a series of pioneering journeys up the Nile and to the Near East.

INTRIGUE AND EXPLORATION

He was the first photographer to venture beyond the sixth cataract of the Nile. Africa was still the mysterious 'Dark Continent', and Stanley and Livingstone's historic meeting was a decade into the future. The conditions for picture taking confound belief. He laboured for hours in his wicker dark-room in the sweltering heat of the desert, while the volatile chemicals fizzed dangerously in their trays. Back in London he exhibited his photographs and was 'rapturously cheered' by members of the Royal Society. His reputation as a photographer was made overnight.

VENTURE OF A LIFE-TIME

By the 1870s the railways had threaded their way across the country, and Bank Holidays and half-day Saturdays had been made obligatory by Act of Parliament. All of a sudden the working man and his family were able to enjoy days out, take holidays, and see a little more of the world.

With typical business acumen, Francis Frith foresaw that these new tourists would enjoy having souvenirs to commemorate their days out. For the next thirty years he travelled the country by train and by pony and trap, producing fine photographs of seaside resorts and beauty spots that were keenly bought by millions of Victorians.

These prints were painstakingly pasted into family albums and pored over during the dark nights of winter, rekindling precious memories of summer excursions. Frith's studio was soon supplying retail shops all over the country, and by 1890 F Frith & Co had become the greatest specialist photographic publishing company in the world, with over 2,000 sales outlets, and pioneered the picture postcard.

FRANCIS FRITH'S LEGACY

Francis Frith had died in 1898 at his villa in Cannes, his great project still growing. The archive he created continued in business for another seventy years. By 1970 it contained over a third of a million pictures showing 7,000 British towns and villages.

Frith's legacy to us today is of immense significance and value, for the magnificent archive of evocative photographs he created provides a unique record of change in the cities, towns and villages throughout Britain over a century and more. Frith and his fellow studio photographers revisited locations many times down the years to update their views, compiling for us an enthralling and colourful pageant of British life and character.

We are fortunate that Frith was dedicated to recording the minutiae of everyday life. For it is this sheer wealth of visual data, the painstaking chronicle of changes in dress, transport, street layouts, buildings, housing, engineering and landscape that captivates us so much today, offering us a powerful link with the past and with the lives of our ancestors.

Computers have now made it possible for Frith's many thousands of images to be accessed almost instantly. The archive offers every one of us an opportunity to examine the places where we and our families have lived and worked down the years. Its images, depicting our shared past, are now bringing pleasure and enlightenment to millions around the world a century and more after his death.

INTRODUCTION

This pocket book is one of a series of photographic anthologies of subjects and themes from British life, history and heritage.

This attractive pocket book contains 50 classic Frith period photographs of railway scenes from England and Wales.

You'll find all types of trains here, including goods trains, express trains, excursion trains, mountain railways, narrow gauge trains, and funicular railways. You will also see railway stations, railway bridges, viaducts and tunnels. Each photograph is accompanied by an informative caption.

Evocative and atmospheric, these stunning images will transport you back into a captivating world of steam.

This photograph shows the Welsh Highland Railway as a steam locomotive bursts through the rocks on the south side of the Aberglaslyn Pass in Snowdonia. The Welsh Highland Railway was constructed in the 1930s to serve the quarries, stretching from Caernarvon to Porthmadog, and although it is used today as a walking trail, part of it has now been re-opened.

This 12-mile long railway was constructed along the south side of the Rheidol in 1901 to transport lead ore from the mines to the harbour, but it became a very popular tourist attraction for those wishing to visit the Devil's Bridge and waterfalls where the line terminated. This view shows a cutting and embankment that is typical of this steep valley-side line.

ABERYSTWYTH,
THE RHEIDOL RAILWAY 1904 57154

2

Askrigg station is on the North Eastern Railway route between Northallerton and a conection with the Midland Railway at Hawes. Askrigg closed to passengers in April 1945, but remained open for goods traffic for another ten years.

A Great Western class
4575 Prairie (2-6-2
wheel arrangement)
loco starts the climb
towards Bampton with
a train from Tiverton to
Morebath Junction.

BAMPTON, THE RAILWAY C1955 B379040

4

This famous bridge spans the Mawddach estuary. A train is heading south. The railway was built as part of the Cambrian Railway, with two stations, Barmouth and Barmouth Junction. Northwards the line went to Harlech and Afonwen, where it joined the L & NWR. The bridge was opened in September 1867, and its original design, as shown in this picture, included rolling sections that could be opened for river traffic.

There was once a railway running down the middle of this street, and around the corner at the end. It went to Westward Ho! and Appledore, and ran for 16 years, closing in March 1917.

The lift railway was still very new when this photograph was taken - it was built in 1891. Rising 111 feet high up the cliff, it is 201 feet long. The town is also a centre for another type of railway - the restored Severn Valley Railway with its steam engines.

BRIDGNORTH, THE LIFT 1898 42631

The pride of the stationmaster at Burry Port is typical of the time - it was considered the stationmaster's duty to make the platform as attractive as possible. This can be seen clearly in the rockery and floral arrangements shown here. The railway line west of Llanelli was the creation of the great days of the coal and tin plate trade.

CAISTER-ON-SEA, THE 'CAMP SPECIAL' ARRIVES C1955

The 'Holiday Camps Express' ran from London to Caister and the other Norfolk holiday camps at California, Scratby and Hemsby every Saturday in summer from 1934 to 1938, and again from 1948 to 1958.

The East Cornwall Mineral Railway, from Kelly Bray, near Callington, to Calstock Quay, opened in 1872, but in 1908 it was re-laid to standard gauge and connected to Plymouth via the Calstock Viaduct. This picture was taken shortly after the opening on 2 March 1908; the locomotive could be the 'Lord St Levan'. This end of the line closed in 1966.

A modest train of the old London & South Western puffs into Calstock station, having crossed the slender viaduct that bridges the Tamar. The journey into Cornwall transported travellers into a land of unique beauty, remote brown stone hamlets and the poignant remains of deserted mines and engine houses.

Cornwall's most westerly branch line, just 4 miles long, was opened from St Erth to St Ives in 1877.

CARBIS BAY, THE SANDS C1955 C22075

12

Clandon station was used by ambulance trains in the Second World War. In 1947 a pre-cast concrete bridge at the opposite end of the station replaced the steel footbridge seen in this photograph.

13

CLANDON, THE STATION 1907 57860X

The first station at Clapham Junction, then known as Falcon Bridge, was opened in 1863, as an interchange station of the London and South Western Railway with the West End and Crystal Palace, the West London Extension and the London Brighton and South Coast Railways. This railway development transformed Battersea and Clapham into residential areas, increasing the population from 6,000 to 168,000 between 1840 and 1910.

In 1932 Corby was chosen to be the site of one of the biggest iron and steel-making complexes in the world. This view is taken from the bridge over Rockingham Road, and shows the four blast furnaces, the Brassert towers (gas cleaners), and the cooling towers of the Stewarts and Lloyds Works, later to become part of the British Steel Corporation. A Barclay saddleback engine can be seen on the right.

Isambard Kingdom Brunel built the famous Box Tunnel in 1841 as part of the Great Western Railway link between London's Paddington station and Bristol's Temple Meads. The 120 miles of railway line took 5 years to complete. Limestone from the excavated tunnel was used for building houses in nearby Corsham.

CORSHAM,
THE BOX TUNNEL 1904 51492

16

After the construction of Corsham's Box Tunnel, the railway was used to transport stone from the local quarries; the town lies on the main London to South Wales line, and had its own station until the Dr Beeching cuts of the 1960s.

The station buildings were demolished at the time of its closure, along with most of the platforms.

CORSHAM, THE MAIL TRAIN 1906 54342

A train approaches the down platform of this station on the Horsham to Guildford Railway, which opened in 1865 and is long since closed. There were five stations, Bramley, Cranleigh, Baynards, Rudgwick and Slinfold. The area is now a car park.

Designed and built by George Stephenson, Stockton & Darlington No 1, 'Locomotion', achieved a maximum speed of 15mph when she hauled the 34-wagon inaugural train from Shildon to Stockton on 27 September 1825. 'Locomotion' was one of the stars of the S & DR centenary celebrations in 1925, though the old girl was not quite herself; her power came from a hidden petrol engine, and the smoke from her chimney was burning oily waste.

Brunel's seaside railway runs in and out of the cliffs though five narrow tunnels, offering a breathtaking ride for travellers to Paignton and Torquay. Both the railway line and the station at Dawlish are right on the beach, exposed to everything the English Channel can throw at them; in severe weather, services are disrupted.

In 1862 the South Eastern Railway extended their track from the Town Station to the Admiralty Pier. The aim was to allow trains to be run onto the pier alongside the cross-Channel steamers, providing a rail connection with London. In 1861 a second rail link with London was opened by the London, Chatham & Dover Railway, and from 1864 boat trains of both companies used Admiralty Pier.

At the time of this photograph the Ravenglass and Eskdale Railway was a commercial 15" gauge passenger train on the line of an old railway originally built to connect the Ironstone mines of the area with the port of Ravenglass. The railway was closed in 1960, and bought at auction by the hurriedly formed Ravenglass and Eskdale Railway Preservation Society.

ESKDALE GREEN, RAVENGLASS AND
ESKDALE RAILWAY c1950 E194071

22

Built around 1840 to carry the London and North Western Railway line north through Lancashire, this splendid six-arch bridge strides across the River Wyre just below Scorton Lakes.

The coming of the Ulverstone and Lancaster Railway, which opened in 1857, led to the building of the promenade alongside it at Grange. Here, a local passenger train is on the up line for Barrow, having left Grange station. On the left is the bandstand: it was removed to that position in 1928 so as to be away from the smuts and noise of the railway.

Gunnislake is set at the heart of an ancient tin mining district. The goods sidings at the station recall Cornwall's past prosperity based on the mining of tin. Above the village are the remains of the mammoth mine of Drake Walls.

The station (which serves the Piccadilly and Metropolitan lines of the London Underground) was moved and re-built in 1992 to accommodate the moving and widening of the A40 Western Avenue. The modern-looking station can be seen from the new road. Metropolitan trains had been serving West London areas like Hillingdon since the late 19th century. The Piccadilly line arrived in the 1930s.

HILLINGDON,
THE RAILWAY STATION c1960 H431034

26

HYTHE AND DYMCHURCH LIGHT RAILWAY 1927 80395

The Romney, Hythe and Dymchurch Railway is said to be the world's smallest public railway service. The 15-inch gauge line opened in 1927. From Hythe to New Romney the line is double tracked, so trains travelling in opposite directions can pass each other. However, beyond New Romney the line is a single track to Dungeness with a passing place at Romney Sands.

Great Western trains thundered through Liskeard bound for Penzance, carrying travellers to within ten miles of Land's End.

The Great Orme Railway, now known as the Great Orme Tramway, is actually two funiculars, end-to-end; the cars are hauled by a single, endless cable driven from the engine house, one car ascending as the other decends.

Corris, which gave its name to the Welsh narrow-gauge railway line, is a slate-quarrying village in the Afon Dulas. The narrow-gauge railway ran from Machynlleth to Corris. It was opened in 1859 and closed, following flooding, in 1948. This locomotive is now used on the Tal-y-Llyn railway.

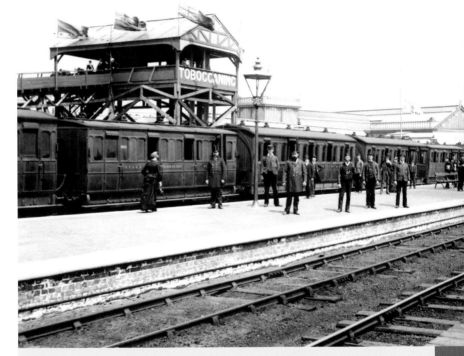

Manchester's Royal Jubilee Exhibition at Old Trafford opened on Tuesday, 2 May 1887. A special railway station served the Exhibition, with a total of 4.75 million visitors recorded over the 166-day period of the event.

MANCHESTER,
EXHIBITION STATION 1887-21904

◀ *A south-bound train thunders across the Monsal Head viaduct. This stately five-arched structure now carries the Monsal Trail; and despite John Ruskin's outbursts when it was built, it is now a protected structure.*

▶ *The locomotive comes tender first into Newby Bridge station, where it is awaited by the station-master. The Ulverston to Lakeside line was built in 1869, but closed and then reopened again in 1965 as a tourist railway. The station buildings have gone, but the line is still open as part of the Lakeside and Haverthwaite Railway.*

NEWBY BRIDGE,
THE PLATFORM 1914 67417

33

Newcastle's Central Station, designed by John Dobson, is seen by many as one of the great monuments of the railway age, a most appropriate achievement since the railway pioneer George Stephenson was born at Wylam, near Newcastle. When the station was completed in 1865 it covered 17 acres and had 2 miles of platforms.

34

NEWCASTLE UPON TYNE,
NEWCASTLE CENTRAL c1960 N16060

A rail connection made with Par in the 1870s gave Newquay direct access from the Great Western Railway, and therefore a boost to the town's potential as a tourist resort. The railway into Newquay crossed the Trenance valley on a viaduct, first with stone piers carrying a timber trestle top, later replaced by iron girders (as seen here) and finally rebuilt with stone arches in 1939.

When this photograph was taken, the trains had only been running on standard gauge track for 15 years. The GWR originally used Brunel's broad gauge, which was just over 7ft, but in order to fall into line with other railways the conversion to standard gauge was made in 1892. The GWR could not afford to stop the trains for too long, and so the whole line was converted in just two days, a feat which borders on the unbelievable, and which must have involved thousands of workers.

NEWTON ABBOT, THE RAILWAY STATION 1907 58430

Romford railway station retained its rural charm until 1930; then, the Romford Railway Improvement Scheme enlarged the buildings to accommodate the growing numbers of commuters. The milk churns are a reminder of how Romford still fed the capital from its farmland and glasshouses.

38   PRESTON, THE RIVER RIBBLE FROM MILLER PARK C1955
P113018

This photograph shows steam engine 'Black 5', the workhorse of the LMS region, heading south with non-corridor stock on a local, probably to Bamber Bridge and on to Blackburn. The railway bridge here was built in 1838 by North Union Railways for the Preston to Wigan line at a cost of £70,000, and is now part of the west coast main line.

Unlike many branch lines throughout Britain, the old Midland Line serving the model factory town of Saltaire between Bradford and Skipton in the Aire Valley has been kept open. Metro diesels are now the order of the day, and a steam loco like the one in this photograph is a rarity.

SALTAIRE, THE RAILWAY STATION 1909 61871

Brunel's celebrated masterpiece across the Tamar estuary made the first direct rail link between Cornwall and the rest of England when it was opened by Prince Albert in May 1859. The bridge is only 31 years old in this view; it is taken from the Cornwall bank, looking towards Plymouth, with Saltash station in the foreground.

◁ There were two stations at Savernake, an Upper and Lower; one served the Great Western Company, the other the Midland SW Junction.

▷ Carlisle and Sons' delivery van waits at the level crossing near Silecroft station on the west coast route between Barrow and Workington, which opened to traffic in 1848.

This 3,650ft-high mountain is the highest in England and Wales. Tourists came to Snowdon in greater numbers after the Snowdon Mountain Railway opened in 1896, which provided easy access to the summit for the holidaymakers. The railway is the only rack railway in Britain, and runs for just over 4.5 miles from Llanberis to Snowdon Summit. This view shows the brand-new locomotive No 3, 'Wyddra' ascending out of Llanberis towards Snowdon - the rack is clearly visible. The line climbs over 3,000ft, with an average gradient of 1 in 7, though parts of the line are 1 in 5.5. Trains only run in summer.

A Great Western steam locomotive hauls the 'Cornish Riviera Express' towards St Austell from Par. The train is seen from the Carlyon Bay golf course near the Crinnis arch. Diesel locomotives made their first appearance in the late 50s and the last steam train ran in 1964.

45

ST BLAZEY, THE STATION 1904   52319A

This view shows two passenger trains in St Blazey station. The train facing the camera is waiting to depart for the Luxulyan valley and Newquay. On the left are the extensive railway workshops erected by the Cornwall Mineral Railway, with the chimneys and waste tips of the old Par Consols Mine on the skyline.

SUTTON-ON-TRENT, THE RAILWAY

This evocative photograph shows an LNER steam locomotive hauling a train of wagons through Sutton-on-Trent station. The steam engines have now departed, and the station has utterly vanished, although the east coast main line itself remains.

Here we see workers leaving the Great Western Railway yard, which at one time employed 12,000 people. The sheer size of the building indicates the importance of the railway to the town. The Great Western Railway had its locomotive works here; some of England's most famous steam engines were made in this factory. As railway services contracted, a major rationalisation in the 1980s saw the unthinkable happen - the Swindon works closed.

Victorian enthusiasm for railways soon ensured that all the major tourist centres of the Isle of Wight could be reached by the Permanent Way. Visitors would often combine the use of a train with cycling or walking as a way of seeing the island.

VENTNOR, THE STATION 1908 60534

To the left of York's city wall stands the station opened by the North Eastern Railway in 1877. To the right of the wall is the original station, which was opened in 1841, and used by the Great North of England and the York & North Midland Railways. The wall had to be breached and an arch built in order to allow the tracks to enter the city.

The magnificent sweep of York station dates from the completion of the Doncaster-Selby-York route. Opened in July 1877, the station allowed through running of trains. The old station it replaced lay just within the city walls; its site and layout were such that trains had either to back in or out of it.

INDEX

FREE PRINT OF YOUR CHOICE

Choose any Frith photograph in this book.

Simply complete the Voucher opposite and return it with your remittance for £2.25 (to cover postage and handling) and we will print the photograph of your choice in SEPIA (size 11 x 8 inches) and supply it in a cream mount with a burgundy rule line (overall size 14 x 11inches).

Please note: photographs with a reference number starting with a "Z" are not Frith photographs and cannot be supplied under this offer.

Offer valid for delivery to UK addresses only.

PLUS: **Order additional Mounted Prints at HALF PRICE - £7.49 each** (normally £14.99)

If you would like to order more Frith prints from this book, possibly as gifts for friends and family, you can buy them at half price (with no additional postage and handling costs).

PLUS: **Have your Mounted Prints framed**

For an extra £14.95 per print you can have your mounted print(s) framed in an elegant polished wood and gilt moulding, overall size 16 x 13inches (no additional postage and handling required).

FRITH PRODUCTS AND SERVICES

All Frith photographs are available for you to buy as framed or mounted prints. From time to time, other illustrated items such as Address Books, Calendars, Table Mats are also available. Already, almost 50,000 Frith archive photographs can be viewed and purchased on the internet through the Frith website.

For more detailed information on Frith companies and products, visit:

www.francisfrith.co.uk

Mounted Print

Overall size 14 x 11 inches (355 x 280mm)

IMPORTANT!

These special prices are only available if you use this form to order. You must use the ORIGINAL VOUCHER on this page (no copies permitted).

We can only despatch to one address. This offer cannot be combined with any other offer.

For further information, contact:

The Francis Frith Collection, Frith's Barn,

Teffont, Salisbury SP3 5QP

Tel: +44 (0) 1722 716 376

Fax: +44 (0) 1722 716 881

Email: sales@francisfrith.co.uk

Voucher

for FREE and Reduced Price Frith Prints

Do not photocopy this voucher. Only the original is valid, so please fill it in, cut it out and return it to us with your order.

Picture ref no	Page number	Qty	Mounted @ £7.49	Framed + £14.95	Order Total £
1		1	Free of charge*	£	£
2			£7.49	£	£
3			£7.49	£	£
4			£7.49	£	£
5			£7.49	£	£
6			£7.49	£	£
			* Post & handling	£2.25	
			Total Order Cost	£	

Please allow 28 days for delivery.

Offer available to one UK address only

Title of this book . . . .

I enclose a cheque / postal order for £ . . . .
payable to 'The Francis Frith Collection'

OR debit my Mastercard / Visa / Maestro

Card Number

Issue No (Maestro only)   Valid from (Maestro)

Expires   Signature

Name Mr/Mrs/Ms . . . .

Address . . . .

. . . . Postcode . . . .

Daytime Tel No . . . .

E-mail . . . .

1-85937-903-6   Valid to 31/12/08